LIGHTNING
BOLT
BOOKS™

The Rocky Mountains

Jeffrey Zuehlke

D1367082

Lerner Publications Company
Minneapolis

For Ellie,
the backbone
of our family

—J.Z.

Lerner Publications Company
A division of Lerner Publishing Group, Inc.
241 First Avenue North
Minneapolis, MN 55401 U.S.A.

Website address: www.lernerbooks.com

Library of Congress Cataloging-in-Publication Data

Zuehlke, Jeffrey, 1968–
    The Rocky Mountains / by Jeffrey Zuehlke.
        p.   cm. — (Lightning bolt books™—famous places)
    Includes index.
    ISBN 978–0–7613–4454–4 (lib. bdg. : alk. paper)
    1. Rocky Mountains—Juvenile literature. 2. Rocky Mountains—Geography—Juvenile literature.
    I. Title.
    F721.Z84 2010
    917.8—dc22   2009017495

Manufactured in the United States of America
1 — BP — 12/15/09

Contents

Welcome to the Rocky Mountains

Have you ever seen these mountains? They are the Rocky Mountains.

Many people call them the Rockies. The Rockies reach from Alaska to New Mexico in the United States. In Canada, they spread through Alberta and British Columbia.

The Rocky Mountain chain is more than 3,000 miles (4,800 kilometers) long.

Several rivers begin in the Rockies. The Arkansas, the Colorado, the Columbia, the Missouri, and the Rio Grande all begin there.

The Colorado River gets its start in the Rocky Mountains. It flows south through the Grand Canyon.

The Rockies make up the Continental Divide. That's an invisible line. It separates eastern and western North America.

People call the Rockies the Backbone of North America. This sign is along the Continental Divide.

LOVELAND PASS
ELEVATION 11,990 FT.

CONTINENTAL
DIVIDE

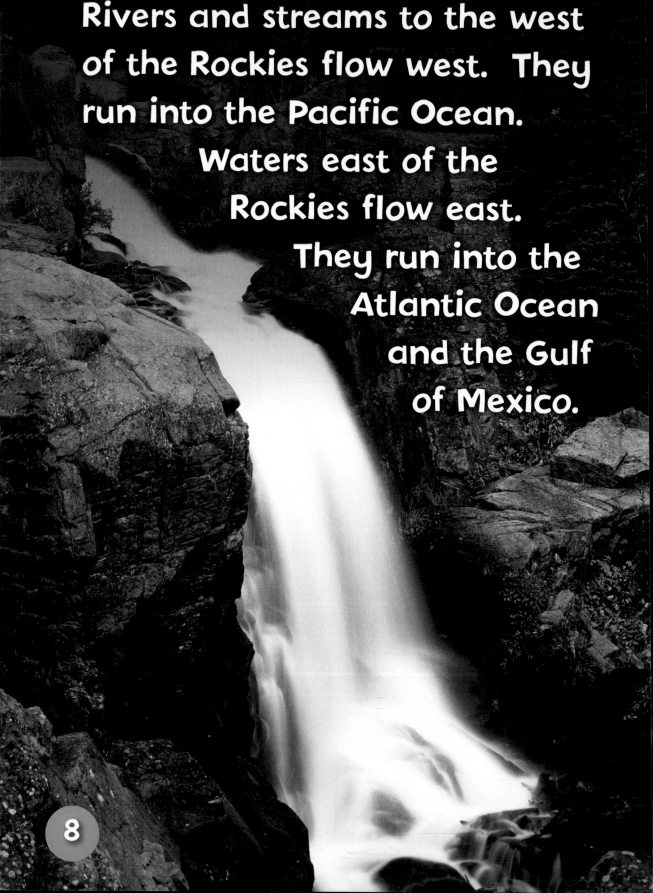

Rivers and streams to the west of the Rockies flow west. They run into the Pacific Ocean. Waters east of the Rockies flow east. They run into the Atlantic Ocean and the Gulf of Mexico.

In the United States, the Rockies cut through Alaska, Washington, Idaho, Montana, Wyoming, Colorado, Utah, and New Mexico.

This green area shows the Rocky Mountains. This photo was taken from far above Earth.

The Rockies are beautiful.
They are home to many plants
and animals.

But how did the mountains form?

10

Building the Rocky Mountains

The Rockies are millions of years old. They formed when huge plates of land pushed together. Over time, they folded over one another.

From far above, the Rocky Mountains look like a lot of folds in Earth's surface.

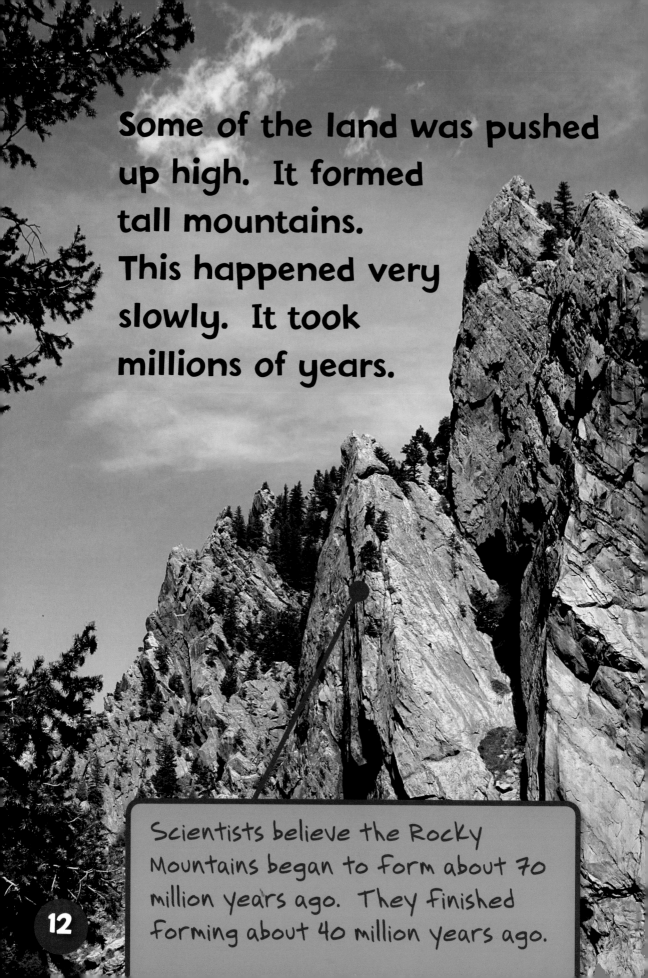

Some of the land was pushed up high. It formed tall mountains. This happened very slowly. It took millions of years.

Scientists believe the Rocky Mountains began to form about 70 million years ago. They finished forming about 40 million years ago.

Other forces also shaped the Rockies. Glaciers helped shape them. Glaciers are giant moving sheets of ice. They move very slowly.

Heavy glaciers carve out land over thousands of years.

Volcanoes helped shape the Rockies too. Volcanoes create lava. The lava flows from the volcano. It piles up. Then it cools. It becomes rock. Over time, layers of lava build up to make mountains.

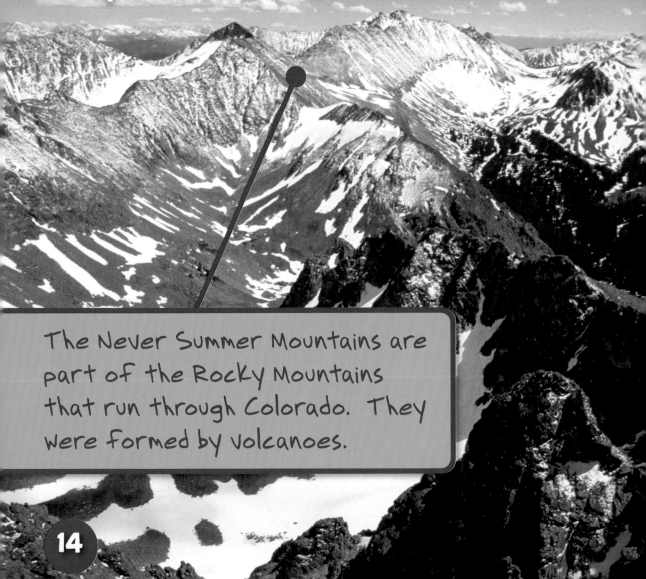

The Never Summer Mountains are part of the Rocky Mountains that run through Colorado. They were formed by volcanoes.

Water also helped form the Rockies. Flowing water slowly wears away land. This is called erosion.

Flowing river water has worn away parts of the Rockies.

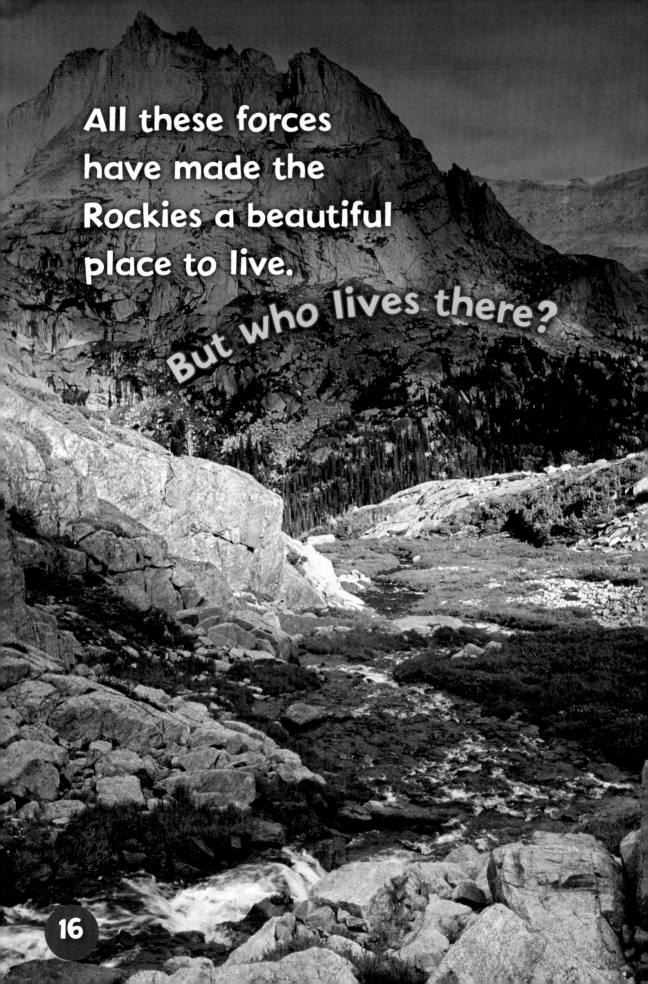

All these forces
have made the
Rockies a beautiful
place to live.

But who lives there?

Life in the Rocky Mountains

The Rockies are home to lots of plants and animals. The tops of the mountains are above the timberline. That's the highest point at which trees can grow on a mountain. This means trees can't grow on the tops of the Rockies. But some plants and animals can live there.

This mountain goat lives high up in the Rockies.

Other animals live in the forested slopes below the timberline.

Bears, deer, mountain lions, hares, and squirrels live here.

Still other animals live in the valleys below. Bison, elk, coyotes, beavers, and raccoons live in the valleys. Birds, such as bald eagles and owls, live here too.

Elk have large antlers on their heads.

Many kinds of fish live in the Rockies. They live in the rivers, streams, lakes, and ponds. Trout, pike, salmon, bass, carp, and catfish all live in these waters.

Trout swim through a stream in the Rocky Mountains.

Turtles, snakes, and frogs also live in the Rockies. Most of them live in or near lakes and streams.

A turtle suns itself on a fallen log.

Many trees, grasses, and flowers grow in the Rockies. Fir, pine, and cedar grow on the mountain slopes.

Many slopes and valleys of the Rocky Mountains are covered with trees.

Lilies, daisies, and sunflowers bloom in spring and summer. All this beauty makes the Rockies a great place to visit.

Red and yellow flowers brighten a green field in the Rockies.

Visiting the Rocky Mountains

The **Rocky Mountains** are home to several national parks. Some of these are in the United States. Others are in Canada. Millions of people visit the parks each year.

Glacier National Park has more than 700 miles (1,127 km) of hiking trails and wooden walkways.

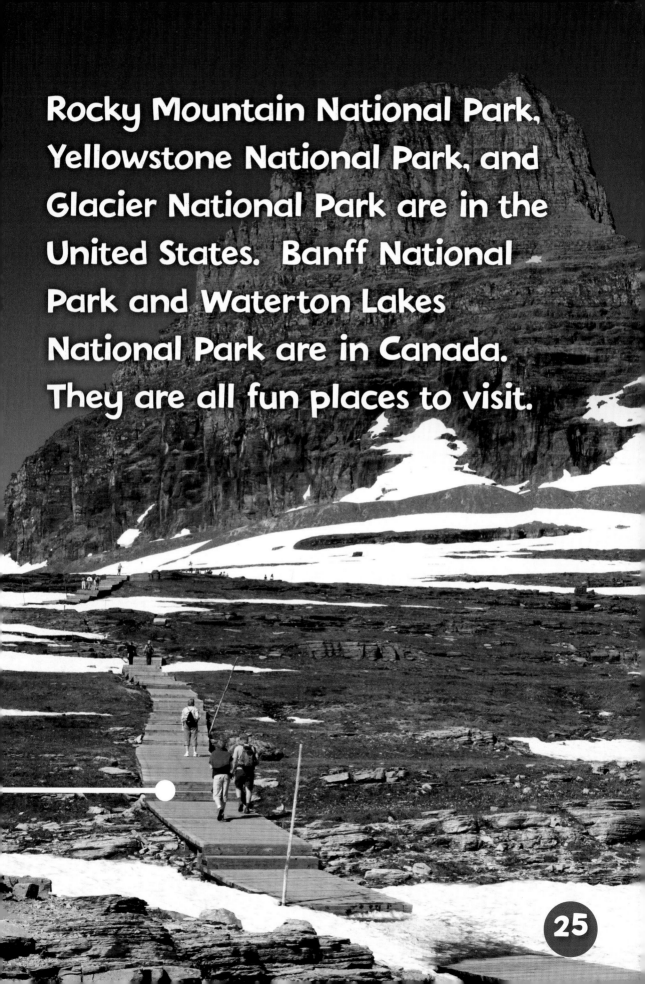

Rocky Mountain National Park, Yellowstone National Park, and Glacier National Park are in the United States. Banff National Park and Waterton Lakes National Park are in Canada. They are all fun places to visit.

About 3 million people visit Rocky Mountain National Park each year. This park is in Colorado. Badgers, beavers, moose, and many other animals live in the park.

Hikers get ready to cross a bridge in Rocky Mountain National Park.

Many people also call the Rockies home. Nearly 8 million people live in the Rocky Mountain states. Are you one of them?

This town is in a valley of the Rocky Mountains.

Rocky Mountain Area

Alaska
(U.S.A.)

R O C K Y   M O U N T A I N S

PACIFIC OCEAN

CANADA

N

Area of
the Rocky
Mountains

UNITED
STATES

Washington

Montana

Idaho

Wyoming

Nevada

Utah

▲ Mount
Elbert

Colorado

UNITED

STATES

Arizona

New
Mexico

MEXICO

Fun Facts

- Humans first began living in the Rocky Mountains around eleven thousand years ago.

- Pikes Peak is one of the most famous mountains in the Rockies. More than half a million people visit this beautiful landmark each year.

- The tallest mountain in the Rockies is Mount Elbert in Colorado. It is 14,440 feet (4,401 meters) above sea level.

- Scientists have discovered hundreds of dinosaur fossils in the Rocky Mountains.

- Denver, Colorado, is the largest city in the Rockies. About 567,000 people live there.

- Yellowstone National Park was the first U.S. national park. The U.S. government made it a park in 1872.

Glossary

Continental Divide: the invisible line that separates eastern and western North America

erosion: the process in which flowing water wears away land

glacier: a giant moving sheet of ice

national park: an area that is owned, protected, and run by a government

slope: ground that is slanted downward

timberline: the highest point at which trees can grow on a mountain

valley: a low area between hills and mountains

volcano: a hole in Earth's surface through which lava, steam, and ash pour out

Further Reading

Mader, Jan. *Rocky Mountains.* New York: Children's Press, 2004.

Rocky Mountain National Park (U.S. National Park Service)
http://www.nps.gov/romo/index.htm

Rocky Mountain Web Ranger Challenge
http://www.heartoftherockies.net/romo_wrc/game.htm

Walker, Sally M. *Glaciers.* Minneapolis: Lerner Publications Company, 2008.

Walker, Sally M. *Volcanoes.* Minneapolis: Lerner Publications Company, 2008.

Index

Photo Acknowledgments

The images in this book are used with the permission of: © Gene Ahrens/SuperStock, pp. 4–5; © Image Source/Getty Images, p. 6; © Kelly Bates/Dreamstime.com, p. 7; © Adam Jones/Visuals Unlimited, Inc., p. 8; NASA/GSFC/LaRC/JPL, MISR Team, p. 9; © age fotostock/SuperStock, pp. 10, 16, 26; © Thinkstock/Getty Images, p. 11; © Joshua Haviv/Dreamstime.com, p. 12; © Svecchiotti/Dreamstime.com, p. 13; © Christopher Alan Selby/Alamy, p. 14; © Don Grall/Visuals Unlimited, Inc., p. 15; © Bambi L. Dingman/Dreamstime.com, p. 17; © Daniel J. Cox/Stone/Getty Images, p. 18; © Barbcovington/Dreamstime.com, p. 19; © Robert & Jean Pollock/Visuals Unlimited, Inc., p. 20; © Rick & Nora Bowers/Alamy, p. 21; © Steve Vidler/SuperStock, p. 22; © Ron Dahlquist/SuperStock, p. 23; © Jim Parkin/Dreamstime.com, p. 25; © Andrew Lundquist/Dreamstime.com, p. 27; © Laura Westlund/Independent Picture Service, p. 28; © J. C. Leacock/Aurora/Getty Images, p. 30; © Linde Waidhofer/Taxi/Getty Images, p. 31.

Front cover: © Philip and Karen Smith/Stone/Getty Images.